HOGARTH'S ENGLAND

A Selection of the Engravings

with descriptive text

by Eveline Cruikshanks

FOLIO SOCIETY, LONDON, 1957

DISTRIBUTED IN THE UNITED STATES
BY PHILIP C. DUSCHNES, NEW YORK

Set in 10 point Baskerville 1 point leaded
Illustrations and text printed by Sun Printers Ltd., Watford
Bound by The Dorstel Press, Harlow
Printed in Great Britain

CONTENTS

INTRODUCTION

Hogarth's prints, which span almost exactly the reign of George II (1727-1760), reflect the earthiness and robust prosperity of the age of Walpole and the self-reliant pride and national greatness of the age of Chatham. Perhaps the most striking feature of the eighteenth-century Englishman was his aggressiveness, his overwhelming sense of superiority over the rest of the world. War was welcome to the English merchant classes as a golden opportunity to seize the wealth and trade of the world, particularly that of their hated rivals across the Channel, the priest-ridden, frog-eating, wooden-clogged French slaves. This feeling Hogarth expressed supremely well in such prints as *The Invasion*, which are pictorial counterparts of the maniac fury of Chatham's denunciations of France and Spain.

The age of British commercial prosperity was also the 'Age of Elegance.' The conversation pieces of the period, a style in which Hogarth excelled, depict magnificent drawing-rooms, where immaculately dressed young men in silks and satins, holding finely chiselled snuff-boxes, converse with exquisitely dressed young women, holding delicate porcelain teacups. The ruling classes, aristocracy and landed gentry, had a taste for architecture and a passion for collecting works of art. Houses designed according to the principles of Palladio, or other Italian masters, as expounded by Lord Burlington, or, more often, by his disciple William Kent, were set in spacious grounds where art and nature were skilfully blended by such masters of landscape gardening as 'Capability' Brown. Their furniture was French, or modelled by English craftsmen in French or Italian styles, their pictures Italian, leaving only portraits to be painted by English artists. The result, though magnificent, was somewhat unoriginal. This infatuation of the upper classes with foreign fashions and foreign masters, which robbed English artists of patronage, infuriated Hogarth, who never failed to satirize it in his prints. Picture-jobbers from abroad, he exclaimed, are 'continually importing ship-loads of dead Christs, Holy Families, Madonnas, and other dismal dark subjects, neither entertaining nor ornamental . . . that grand Venus (as you are pleased to call it) has not beauty enough for the character of an English cook-maid.'

In Hogarth's prints we see the extraordinary mixture of splendour and squalor that was eighteenth-century London. Its narrow courts and alleys, its cobbled streets, creaking sign-boards and oil-lamps, as well as its taverns, coffee-houses and brothels in Covent Garden and Drury Lane, come to life before our eyes. London was a city of abrupt transition from the dark alleys and rookeries of the river banks and Lime House in the south and east to the fine new residential areas in West London: Cavendish, Hanover, Grosvenor and Berkeley Squares. In the midst of elegance and luxury, dirt and disease abounded. The savage pictures Hogarth drew of the London poor are far closer records of Georgian society than the picture of the fashionable world drawn from society diarists. The mass of the population was in casual employment, alternating between modest prosperity and abject poverty, and their hard lean faces and shrunken bodies give a sense of bitter despair to many of Hogarth's prints. London was full of slums; the abominable tenements of St Giles, Drury Lane, Shoreditch, and Alsatia, where human beings swarmed in dark cellars and tumbling attics. As an anodyne for their misery, the poor turned to drink, especially to gin, which was cheap and abundant, and to savage amusements, such as cock-fighting, bear- and bull-baiting, and the most ferocious kind of prize-fighting. Rioting was a favourite pastime, since it afforded easy loot, and disorders of all kinds were rife. The state machinery to deal with them was feeble and inefficient; parish-constables, narrowly circumscribed in their functions, were pitifully inadequate against riots, and not numerous enough to secure the speedy arrest of highwaymen, footpads, pickpockets and other petty thieves infesting the streets. The government were driven to imposing increasingly severe penalties against crime—a child could be hanged for stealing a handkerchief—but largely ineffectively. Against the prevailing callous attitude to life and indifference to punishment, Hogarth made a very effective protest. His campaign against gin-drinking in *Gin Lane*, against cruelty and crime in *The Four Stages of Cruelty* and *Industry and Idleness*, did much to educate the poor, and the marked improvement in behaviour and conditions of life generally in the second half of the eighteenth century owes much to him, as well as to his friend, the novelist and magistrate, Henry Fielding. Between 1720 and 1750 there were twice as many burials as baptisms in London, and the resulting depopulation was due largely to an orgy of gin. Employers sold gin to their work-people or even paid their wages in the form of drink. Large fortunes were made in the distilling trade, which was regarded as the great support of the landed interest because it used up their corn surpluses. Death reaped the richest harvest of all. Legislation against this evil had been largely ineffective until the passing of the Gin Act in 1751 which marked a turning point in the social history of London.

Hogarth was born on 10 November, 1697, the son of an impoverished school-master, who ran a school in Ship Close, near the Old Bailey. At his own request, he was apprenticed to a silver-plate engraver, subsequently turning to copper-plate engraving; by 1720 he was in business on his own account, engraving shop-bills and plates for booksellers. At this time, he began to attend a private art school run by the painter Sir James Thornhill, for whom he had a great admiration. Their intimacy, however, was interrupted in 1729 by Hogarth's elopement and private marriage with Thornhill's daughter Jane, a handsome young woman of 19. The resounding success of *A Harlot's Progress* (1732), Hogarth's first major work, brought about a reconciliation with his father-in-law, who declared 'Very well; the man who can furnish representations like these, can also maintain a wife without a portion.' *A Harlot's Progress* was the rage of the day, being set to music, used as decorations for teacups and fans, and so on; yet Hogarth lost much of the benefit of this tremendous popularity because of the flood of pirated copies of his prints issued by Grub Street booksellers. He and his friends petitioned Parliament to correct this abuse, and in 1735 an Act was passed vesting in designers and engravers an exclusive right to their own works, and restraining the multiplication of copies without their consent. In the same year, after the passing of this Act, Hogarth published *A Rake's Progress* which, in spite of its excellence, did not enjoy the same vogue as its predecessor, probably because it satirized so effectively the prevailing vices of the ruling classes. In 1745 Hogarth issued the series then and subsequently regarded as his masterpiece, *Marriage à la Mode*, and in 1749 engraved his own self-portrait, with his dog Trump, one of the most successful of his works. The portrait gives an excellent index to the artist's character: a sturdy, outspoken, honest, obstinate, pugnacious little man.

A self-made man, Hogarth had won for himself a unique position, completely apart from the art-fraternity of his time. His idea of stories in pictures, compared by Horace Walpole to Molière's comedies, was entirely novel. 'I wished', wrote Hogarth, 'to compose pictures on canvas, similar to representations on the stage . . . I have endeavoured to treat my subject as a dramatic writer; my picture is my stage, and men and women my players, who by means of certain actions and gestures are to exhibit a *dumbshow*.' For years he had been in the habit of making rapid thumbnail sketches of people and incidents which interested him for future reference, and this enabled him to cram immense richness of detail in his prints, which will repay careful study a hundredfold. 'It was reserved to Hogarth', remarked Horace Walpole, 'to write a scene of furniture. The rake's levee-room, the nobleman's dining-room, the apartments of the husband and wife in *Marriage à la Mode*, the Alderman's parlour, the poet's bedchamber, and many others, are the history of the manners of the age.'

Hogarth's intransigence had made him many enemies among art critics and fellow-

8

artists, who awaited a favourable opportunity to humble him. In his self-portrait, he had introduced a serpentine line on his palette, mysteriously called the 'Line of Beauty and Grace,' which greatly mystified his contemporaries. To satisfy their curiosity, he published in 1753 an ambitious treatise entitled *The Analysis of Beauty*, 'to fix the fluctuating ideas of taste,' professing to define the principle of beauty and grace, and taking for his text his famous serpentine line. The idea was brilliant, but Hogarth had not the literary gifts or precision of mind to save him from confusion in presenting his case, and he laid himself open to endless ridicule. Worse was to follow. By a curious perversion, his desire for distinction seemed to lay in the direction of history-painting as practised by Thornhill. Earlier, in 1736, he had made an attempt in this line by decorating the great staircase of St Bartholomew's Hospital with biblical scenes in 'figures seven feet high,' but meeting with no success abandoned the attempt. In 1759 his many enemies found his Achilles heel at last when he relapsed into an attempt at painting in the 'Grand Manner.' This was the ill-fated *Sigismunda*, inspired by Dryden's story after Boccaccio of a woman weeping over the heart of her murdered lover, and commissioned by a private patron who eventually refused to accept it. This gave rise to a torrent of malicious comment, all the more wounding to the artist since his own wife had been the model. In the last years of his life Hogarth was constantly under attack. He made the grievous mistake of producing his first political print in 1762 when he took up the cudgels on behalf of George III and his inept adviser Lord Bute by publishing *The Times*, a rather confused satire on the opposition, singling out Chatham, Temple, John Wilkes and the polemicist Charles Churchill. Wilkes, whose *North Briton* was the most outspoken newspaper of the time, and Churchill retaliated with an indictment of the alleged failure of Hogarth's powers as an artist, the absurdities of the *Analysis*, and the fiasco of *Sigismunda*, all discussed with merciless malignity. Hogarth, who was in poor health, was deeply hurt. He replied with a rather ineffective satirical portrait of Churchill and with the famous portrait of Wilkes which will ever carry his satyr leer and hideous squint to posterity. This was the last roar of the old lion, for Hogarth never completely recovered, and died on 25 November, 1764.

1697 born
1729 married
1732 "A Harlot's Progress"
1735 Licensing Act "A Rake's Progress"
1738 - Four Times of the Day "
1745 - Marriage à la Mode"

1751 Gin Act passed; Beer Street, Gin Lane
1753 "The Analysis of Beauty"

1759 "Sigismunda"

1764 portrait of Wilkes, dies

A HARLOT'S PROGRESS

A HARLOT'S PROGRESS: 'Wm Hogarth inv^t pinx^t et sculp^t (1734)'

The prints were offered for subscription in 1733, their success being so great that over twelve hundred names were inscribed in the artist's book.

1 *Her arrival in London*

To BELL INN YARD, in Wood Street, Cheapside, has arrived the heavy, lumbering York waggon bringing a fresh country girl to London (York had the reputation of producing very handsome women). The initials on her trunk stand for Moll Hackabout, a reference to the notorious prostitute Kate Hackabout, 'a woman voted in and about the Hundreds of Drury for being a very termagant, and a terror, not only to the civil part of the neighbourhood by her frequent fighting, noise and swearing in the streets in the night-time, but also to other women of her profession,' whose brother had been executed at Tyburn for highway robbery. Moll, still innocent, carries a goose in a basket labelled 'for my lofing cosen in Tems Street in London.'

Her father, the gaunt clergyman on a white, half-starved horse, who has also come to London to make his fortune, is reading a letter of recommendation to a bishop. Ladies wishing to engage maid servants used to meet the waggon, as indeed did procuresses in search of new faces. Here the country girl is being cajoled with flattering promises for the future by the most notorious of them, Mother Needham, seen here as a simpering old woman dressed in a velvet mantle and voluminous satin skirts. Mother Needham, described by a contemporary as 'a matron of great fame and very religious in her ways; whose constant prayer it was that she might get enough by her profession to leave it off in time, and make her peace with God,' kept a fashionable establish-

13

11 *The Quarrel with her Jew Protector*

ment in Park Place, St James's. (Her wish
was never fulfilled for she died just before
the publication of this print, after being
committed to the Gatehouse Prison for
keeping a disorderly house and being
mercilessly pelted in the pillory by the
angry populace.) She was apparently act-
ing here, not on her own account, but on
behalf of the sly old man leaning on a stick
in the doorway of the inn: the sinister
Colonel Francis Charteris or Chartres,
like Mother Needham recently dead. Dismissed from his regiment for card-sharp-
ing, imprisoned for rape at Newgate, a
money lender at exorbitant rates, his
residence 'a perpetual bawdy house,' his
name had become a synonym for unmiti-
gated villainy. 'Francis Chartres,' ran a
satirical epitaph by Arbuthnot, 'who with

an inflexible constancy and inimitable uni-
formity of life persisted in spite of age and
infirmities, in the practice of every human
vice, excepting prodigality and hypocrisy.
His insatiable avarice exempted him from
the first; his matchless impudence from
the second.' Chartres made it his practice
to post his agents at inn-yards—in this
case his confidant 'trusty Jack,' the pimp
John Gourlay—to pick up girls fresh from
the country and engage them as servants
in his own house.

Old libertines never keep women long,
and Moll, now a woman of the world,
becomes the mistress of a rich Jew. It is
the eternal story: her protector is rich but
not young; she has a lover, young but not
rich. The Jew has come to join her at
breakfast unexpectedly early, and she pro-

14

III *Apprehended by a Magistrate*

duces a diversion by petulantly kicking over the tea-table, laden with precious egg-shell china; as the merchant stares, startled and indignant, and the negro page gapes in alarm, the lover, a lithe young French dancing-master, is spirited from the room by her maid.

3 Dismissed by the Jew, no longer a fashionable courtesan but a common prostitute, Moll exchanges her elegant apartment for a miserable garret in Drury Lane, the quarter of which Gay wrote:

O may thy virtue guard thee thro' the roads
Of Drury's mazy courts and dark abodes!
The harlot's guileful paths who nightly stand
Where Catherine Street descends into the Strand.

A broken mirror lies on the table, and round the room are strewn tobacco-pipes, gin-measures and pewter pots, sufficiently indicative of the company she now keeps. Ominous medicine bottles stand on the window-sill above a print of Macheath, the highwayman hero of *The Beggar's Opera*, and another of Dr Sacheverell, the turbulent spokesman of the High Tories. Half hidden from sight, lies the wig-box of a real highwayman, James Dalton, one of the most astute street thieves in London, whose lewdness and audacity was legendary; three times transported to Virginia, he always contrived to escape, but was finally hanged at Tyburn in 1730. From the witch's hat and broom on the wall, Moll appears to frequent masquerades, a favourite entertainment with harlots. By a humorous touch, Hogarth made the wrapping of her pat of butter the Pastoral

IV *Scene in Bridewell*

Letter of Dr Gibson, Bishop of London, a cleric known for his denunciation of masquerades and similar amusements. As Moll examines a watch stolen from or given by last night's client, the stern figure of Sir John Gonson, 'the harlot-hunting justice,' appears suddenly on the scene, accompanied by a troop of constables. Gonson, a puritanical Westminster magistrate, had just undertaken a severe campaign against 'night cellars,' 'night houses' and 'disorderly houses.' When this print first appeared, the Lords of the Treasury were so delighted on being shown Gonson's portrait, that they curtailed their meeting in order to repair to the print-shop to secure copies of their own.

Committed to Bridewell, a house of correction in Tothill Fields, where prostitutes,

vagrants and runaway apprentices were sentenced to short terms of imprisonment, Moll Hackabout, in a flowered petticoat, a remnant of her former magnificence, is set to beating hemp with a heavy wooden mallet. Her feeble efforts are watched disapprovingly by an angry warder standing at her side, and about to strike her with a large rattan. One of the sights of eighteenth-century London was watching women flogged at the Bridewell. Prisoners, whether men or women, were tied to whipping posts, bare to the waist, and whipped before the Court of Governors. The president sat with his hammer in his hand, and the culprit was not taken down until the hammer fell. When women were flogged, the cries 'knock,' 'knock' were loud and incessant. In the background of Hogarth's

v *Expires, while the Doctors are Quarrelling*

print, a lad too idle to work is seen standing on tiptoe to reach the stocks in which his hands are fixed, while over his head is written, 'better to work than stand thus.'

5   In the next scene, several years have elapsed after Moll's release from Bridewell; she has given birth to a little boy, and fallen into great misfortune. Disease has taken its toll; wrapped in loose robes, emaciated and in an agony of pain, she is dying. Two quacks are so engrossed in a violent argument about the niceties of the case, that they have no time to look at their patient. The taller of the two is the irascible Dr John Misaubin, son of a Huguenot clergyman, and specialist in the treatment of venereal diseases, and the other, his gold-headed cane in hand, the plump, self-satisfied, Dr Joshua Ward,

inventor of the famous pill immortalized in *Tom Jones* as 'flying at once to the particular part of the Body on which you desire to operate.' On the floor lies an advertisement for an 'Anodyne Necklace,' which was supposed to be 'the great Specifick Remedy for the Secret Disease.' In the room all is noise, heat, dirt and confusion. The maid begs the two quacks to cease quarrelling, and the nurse plunders the last few possessions of the dying woman from her trunk. The sickly little boy, no doubt accustomed to fend for himself, tries to roast a lump of meat twirling on a string.

  The burial scene gave Hogarth an op- 6 portunity to satirize mercilessly the senseless funeral ceremonial of his day. It was then the custom to have as grand a funeral

17

VI *The Funeral*

as possible, and if the mourners lived near a cemetery, they would take a devious route so as to regale neighbouring streets with their sumptuous procession. Nothing has been neglected for the harlot's funeral: sprigs of rosemary for remembrance, yew to keep infection out, white gloves for the women and black bands for the men, not to mention endless glasses of gin. The bawds of Drury Lane are all gathered here, lachrymose and tipsy; only the serving-woman, who has seen Moll die, shows real grief. The child, dressed as chief mourner, and blissfully unaware of what is going on, plays with his new spinning-top. The seedy Fleet chaplain, a performer of clandestine marriages, who will conduct the funeral service, spills his drink as he fumbles in his neighbour's skirts beneath the cover of his mourning hat. The mercer, or undertaker, stares gloatingly at a female, on whose hand he is fitting a long glove, while, on a stool, a stout Irishwoman wails loudly. The inscription on the coffin reads: 'M. Hackabout. Died Sepr. 1731 aged 23.' It was the utter wastefulness of her life rather than any intrinsic wickedness on her part that stirred Hogarth's indignation.

18

THE FOUR TIMES
OF THE DAY

THE FOUR TIMES OF THE DAY: 'Invented Painted Engrav'd & Publish'd by
W^m. Hogarth March 25 1738 according to Act of Parliament.'
    Advertised together with Strolling Actresses dressing in a Barn (see p. 74) in The London
Daily Post for 4 May 1738 at £1 5s. for the set of five.

1 Morning

MORNING shows Covent Garden very early on a crisp winter day. The market women have arrived with baskets and lanterns, and two little schoolboys slowly and reluctantly wend their way to school. On the left, a quack named Dr Rock holds up a board advertising a universal panacea. On the right, inside Tom King's, the coffee house 'well known to all gentlemen to whom beds are unknown,' a brawl is in progress. One of the night-houses of Covent Garden market and little more than a shed, Tom King's presented a curious spectacle in the morning when 'noblemen and the first beaux after leaving court . . . in full dress with swords and rich brocaded silk coats' mixed freely with chimney-sweeps, gardeners and market people. Two pretty girls are receiving the embraces of a pair of young rakes who have just staggered out, watched by the central figure, a prudish old maid on her way to morning service at Inigo Jones'

21

church of St Paul. This figure inspired
Cowper's verses:

Yon ancient prude, whose wither'd features show
She might be young some forty years ago,
Her elbows pinioned close upon her hips,
Her head erect, her fan upon her lips,
Her eyebrows arched, her eyes both gone astray
To watch yon amorous couple in their play.

She was believed to have been one of
Hogarth's aunts, who, recognizing the
likeness, cut him out of her will.

Noon gives an impression of London's
French Huguenot colony, which had been
steadily increasing since the Revocation of
the Edict of Nantes in 1685 had deprived
French Protestants of civil rights. The congregation is filing out of the French chapel
in Hog Lane, Westminster, with St Giles
Church seen in the distance. It is headed
by a French coxcomb, his wife and a stout
child, all dressed in the latest Paris fashions.
A little boy, who had fetched the Sunday
meal from the pieshop, as was often the

III *Evening*

custom, has broken his dish and is wailing in uproarious misery, as a small pauper girl hungrily snatches the remnants.

The scene of *Evening* is New River, opposite Sadler's Wells, a rural suburb on the North side of London, and a favourite resort of Londoners who sought its tea-gardens and music in a setting of tall poplars, graceful willows and sloping banks of flowers. On a fine summer evening, a group of men are smoking energetically and drinking punch by the open window of the Sir Hugh Middleton, a suburban public house. A London dyer has just arrived, footsore and weary, accompanied by his stout, sweating wife and their offspring out for a breath of country air. One little girl has fallen fast asleep in the arms of her father. The little boy, indulging in a fit of tantrums, is being taken to task by his peevish sister. To heighten the effect of general family harmony, Hogarth arranged the horns of a grazing cow to appear as if sprouting from the dyer's wig.

23

IV *Night*

Night takes place on Restoration Day, 29 May, as indicated by the oaken boughs which decorate the barber's sign and the oak leaves fixed in the hats of passers-by. It is a sultry moonlit night, and between the Rummer Tavern and the Cardigan's Head, two well-known bagnios in the narrowest part of Charing Cross, congestion is at its worst. The Salisbury Flying Coach has overturned in a bonfire in the middle of the road, and, as its frightened passengers struggle out, an intoxicated freemason, wearing the emblem of his craft, who is being led home by a tyler of his lodge, is soused by a chamber-pot emptied from a first-floor window. The Mason has been identified as being Sir Thomas de Veil, Fielding's predecessor at Bow Street, a magistrate whose dissipations demanded a close attention to the profits of office, and who, though intelligent and able, was consequently unpopular. In the distance can be seen the equestrian statue of Charles I.

24

THE FOUR STAGES
OF CRUELTY

THE FOUR STAGES OF CRUELTY: 'Designed by W. Hogarth. Published according to Act of Parliament Feb. 1 1751. Price 1s. 6d.' [each print].

1 *First Stage of Cruelty*

HOGARTH's aim in *The Four Stages of Cruelty* was less artistic than humanitarian. It was a symptom of a new spirit, a revulsion against cruelty to animals, which was altogether novel. 'The leading points', he wrote, 'were made as obvious as possible, in the hope that their tendency might be seen by men of the lowest rank. Neither minute accuracy of design, nor fine engraving, were deemed necessary, as the latter would render them too expensive for the persons to whom they were intended to be useful. . . The prints were engraved in the hope of, in some degree, correcting that barbarous treatment of animals, the very sight of which renders our metropolis so distressing to every feeling mind. If they have had this effect, and checked the progress of cruelty, I am more proud of having been the author, than I should be of having painted Raffaele's Cartoons.' The prints have all the downright power of Hogarth at his best, but, unrelieved as they are by humour of any kind, they tend to be painful and even repulsive.

27

II *Second Stage of Cruelty*

The story opens in St Giles', a district peopled mainly by Irish immigrants, where herds of men behaved little better than savages. Tom Nero, its hero, is a boy of St Giles' Charity School (charity schools were founded under Queen Anne to educate the children of the poor in reading, writing, and the principles of the Church of England). He begins his career by torturing a stray dog held down by one of his accomplices, while a young passer-by, horrified at his barbarity, offers a pastry to Nero as a bribe to stop. All kinds of experiments in cruelty are being practised: a boy is tying a bone to the tail of a dog; two

other brats burn out the eyes of a bird. A pair of young sadists have tied two cats at the extremities of a rope and hung it over a lamp iron, gleefully watching the animals tearing each other to pieces. Humanitarian verses by the Reverend James Townley were engraved below the design.

The next scene is laid at the gate of Thavies Inn, Holborn, a small inn of Chancery mainly taken up by Welsh attorneys. Nero, now a hackney coachman (carmen were reputed to be an ill-mannered set), has been engaged by four barristers, seen here in wigs and gowns, to drive them to Westminster Hall, where

III *Cruelty in Perfection*

most legal business was then transacted. The worn-out horse has collapsed under their weight, overturned the carriage, and broken its leg, whereupon its driver beats it savagely on the head. The man writing is a humanitarian taking down the number of Nero's vehicle so that he may be punished. Several other examples of barbarity are shown: a drover beats an expiring lamb and the driver of a dray sleeps on while his vehicle runs over a boy. An overladen ass, a bull tossing a boy, and bills advertising cock-fighting and Broughton's amphitheatre for boxing complete the picture.

It is a moonlit night in a churchyard, a screech-owl and a bat hover over the mangled corpse of a girl far advanced in pregnancy. Nero, having seduced a servant-girl and persuaded her to rob her mistress, has collected the loot and murdered her. Her cries have raised the alarm, and the murderer has been seized by a group of men armed with pitchforks and staves, who discover her last letter in his pocket:

Dear Tommy,

My mistress has been the best of women to me, and my conscience flies to my face as often as I think of wronging her, yet I am

29

IV *The Reward of Cruelty*

resolved to venture body and soul to do as you would have me so don't fail to meet me as you said you would, for I shall bring along with me all the things I can lay my hands on. So no more at present but I remain yours till death. Ann Gill

In the final scene, Nero's corpse is stretched out on a slab in the lecture room of Surgeons' Hall, in Monkwell Street. Under a recent Act of Parliament, the bodies of criminals, after hanging, were delivered for dissection. The body, a hangman's rope still around its neck, is being worked on by three aproned men, under the cold scientific scrutiny of the anatomists. The demonstrator pointing to Nero's intestine has been identified as John Freke, a famous surgeon, formerly a friend of Hogarth, but with whom the artist had quarrelled. The two skeletons were those of James Field, an eminent pugilist, and Maclean, 'The Gentleman Highwayman,' son of a Presbyterian minister, who lodged in St James's Street near White's and was executed at Tyburn on 3 October 1750 before a crowd of 3,000 people.

THE ELECTION

FOUR PRINTS OF AN ELECTION: 'Painted by W^m. Hogarth and Engraved by W^m. Hogarth, C. Grignion, Le Cave and F. Aviline. Published 24 Feb^{ry}. 1755 (Plate I), 20 Feb^{ry}. 1757 (Plate II), 20 Feb^{ry}. 1758 (Plate III), and 1 Jan^{ry}. 1758 (Plate IV), as the Act directs.'

Subscriptions for the election series were started by Hogarth on 28 March, 1754, at fifteen shillings for the first print, and sixteen shillings and sixpence more for a further three.

1 *An Election Entertainment*

THE 1750's were years of political quietude in England. The failure of the 1745 rebellion had dashed the last hopes of the Jacobites and extreme Tories. Henry Pelham and his brother, the Duke of Newcastle, by conciliation, and by a judicious distribution of vast government patronage, had succeeded in soothing the bitter quarrels which had divided the Whigs in the last years of Sir Robert Walpole's administration (1733-1742). The opposition, or 'country party,' composed mainly of independent country gentlemen, whether Tories or disaffected Whigs, was not organized, and mouthed its old slogans against standing armies, placemen, high taxes and a pro-Hanoverian foreign policy with less and less conviction. This atmosphere of general political tranquillity formed the setting of the Oxfordshire election of 1754 which inspired Hogarth's *Four Prints of an Election*, and which engrossed national attention, not only because of the extraordinary violence and expense it entailed, but even more because it represented an attack by a Whig, the Duke of Marlborough, upon a county which was the last bastion of Jacobitism in England. Hogarth, however, did not set out to give a literal representation of a particular election, but of electioneering in general, and he conveys admirably the rough and tumble, bribery and corruption, atmosphere. He also indicates the chief issues of the 1754 electoral campaign. The first was the notorious Jew Bill of 1753, a measure designed to enable foreign Jews resident in England to become naturalized by Act of Parliament, subject to the same limitations as Jews born in England. The Act aroused the fiercest controversy, and

33

its opponents denounced the exploitation of English Christians by Jewish landlords, which they thought would result. In the first scene Hogarth introduced a procession of 'Old Interest' supporters, seen through the open window, carrying the effigy of the Duke of Newcastle, on whose breast is written 'No Jews.' A banner reading 'Marry and multiply in spite of the devil and the court' alludes to the recent Marriage Act, introduced by Lord Chancellor Hardwicke, to suppress irregular marriages. This ended the scandal of 'Fleet' marriages, whereby unscrupulous parsons, some not even in regular orders, haunted the purlieus of the prison, marrying any couple for a small fee.

The scene within takes place in a country inn where the 'New Interest' is standing treat in one of those popular orgies that threatened to overwhelm its promoters. At the head of the table, one of the candidates, a young man called Richard Slim, submits to the lascivious caresses of a stout lady. On his left, his fellow candidate, Sir Commodity Taxem, is being toasted by a drunken sweep, while a lean barber puffs smoke in his eyes. At the foot of the table, the chairman has fallen into apoplexy from a surfeit of oysters, and the electioneering agent has been stunned by a brickbat thrown from without, the compliment being vigorously returned from within. At the back, a squinting but incorruptible Methodist tailor refuses to take a bribe, in spite of the entreaties of his wife. In the foreground, a butcher with *pro patria* upon his cap pours gin into the green wound of a wincing 'bludgeon man'; Hogarth wrote: 'These two patriots who, let what party will prevail, can be no gainers, yet spend their time which is their fortune, for what

34

III *The Polling*

they suppose right, and for a glass of gin lose their blood, and sometimes their lives, in support of the cause, are, as far as I can see, entitled to an equal portion of fame with many of the emblazoned heroes of ancient Rome.'

Under the 'bludgeon man's' feet is a flag captured from the other party, with the inscription, 'Give us back our eleven days,' a reference to the Act passed in 1752 adopting the Gregorian Calendar, and by which, according to popular prejudice, the Englishman's life-span had been shortened by eleven days.

The next episode, 'Canvassing for votes,' takes place in a country village. On an election showcloth which hangs before the Royal Oak inn on the right, a stream of secret service money is seen issuing from the Treasury, and in the lower compartment Punch, 'ministerial candidate for Guzzledown,' scatters the golden shower among eager electors. Money is being pressed into a farmer's palms by representatives of both parties. Behind, an electioneering agent, 'Mr Tim Partytool,' endeavours to secure the support of the young women on the balcony, with the aid of gifts chosen from a Jew pedlar's tray. The landlady greedily counts her gains, watched by an envious grenadier. The Crown inn in the background, which is also the Excise office, is being besieged by an opposition mob ready to sack it. A cobbler listens to the reminiscences of a sailor who, as the inscription on his mug shows, was at the capture of Porto Bello effected in 1739 by Admiral Vernon, thereafter Britain's most fêted hero.

Polling day has come at last. The 'reserve voters,' consisting of the blind, the dying and the mad, are being hustled to

35

IV *Chairing the Members*

the polling booth. The foremost voter is an old pensioner, who has lost a leg and both arms in Queen Anne's wars, and lays his iron hook upon the Bible. A clerk laughs derisively as lawyers argue over the validity of his oath. Next to him, an idiot with a bib votes at the prompting of a man in fetters, the notorious Dr Shebbeare, who had been imprisoned for libelling George II, and whose sixth 'Letter to the people of England' protrudes from his pocket. On the top of the steps, a dying man, wrapped in a blanket, is being carried by two porters, followed by a blind man and a cripple. Under a bridge in the background, in the course of an uproarious electioneering procession, Britannia's coach is reeling precariously while its unconcerned driver and a foot-man play cards upon the box.

In the last scene, the victorious candidate is being carried in triumphal procession. Hogarth portrayed him in the shape of the much-ridiculed place-hunter and borough-monger, Bubb Dodington, who had failed to secure his re-election at Bridgwater. The back stroke of a flail, wielded by a thresher in front, strikes one of the chair-bearers and causes the unhappy member to cling desperately to his tottering seat. In the house, which is the committee room of the defeated candidates, the leaders of the 'New Interest,' including the Duke of Newcastle, watch from the window. Outside, a crowd follows in the distance, bearing the second member, whose shadow is projected on to the side of a building at the back. A goose hovers over the fat member's head, in parody of the eagle above the laurelled head of Alexander in Le Brun's painting *The Battle of the Granicus.*

36

A RAKE'S PROGRESS

A RAKE'S PROGRESS: '*Invented Painted Engrav'd & Publishd by W^m. Hogarth June the 25 1735. According to Act of Parliament.*'

Advertised in The London Evening Post *for 3 June 1735:* '*The Nine Prints, from the Paintings of Mr Hogarth, one representing a Fair [Southwark Fair, see p. 71] and the others a Rake's Progress, are now printing off, and will be ready to be delivered on the 25th instant. Subscriptions will be taken at Mr Hogarth's, the Golden Head, in Leicester-fields, till the 23rd of June, and no longer, at half a guinea to be paid on subscribing, and half a guinea more on delivery of the prints at the time above mentioned; after which the price will be two guineas, according to the Proposal.—N.B. Mr Hogarth was, and is, obliged, to defer the publication and delivery of the abovesaid Prints till the 25th of June, in order to secure his property, pursuant to an Act lately passed both Houses of Parliament, to secure all new-invented Prints that shall be published after the 24th instant, from being copied without consent of the proprietor, and thereby preventing a scandalous and unjust custom (hitherto practised with impunity) of making and vending base copies of original Prints, to the manifest injury of the Author, and the great discouragement of the arts of Printing and Engraving.*'

1 *The Young Heir takes possession of the Miser's Effects*

ARAKE'S PROGRESS is the timeless story of the young man irrevocably bent on the task of self-destruction. More loosely constructed than its predecessor, *A Harlot's Progress*, it is even more richly illustrated with references to the contemporary scene.

Just up from Oxford University, Tom Rakewell has entered upon his inheritance. His father, a squalid old usurer, who repaired his shoes with soles hacked out of an ancient family Bible, has left a jumble of mortgages, bonds and indentures strewn over the dilapidated room, where an old woman lights a fire in the long-empty grate. While the knavish attorney making the inventory robs the young heir, an undertaker's man, hanging the black hangings intended to be used for the funeral, accidentally uncovers yet another hoard of coins. As he was being fitted for his suit of mourning, Rakewell was interrupted by Sarah Young, a girl he had seduced while at University, who reminds him of his promise of marriage. Rather ineffectively, he tries to stave off the girl's tears and her mother's abuse by offering a handful of coins.

The Levee scene sees the transformation of the clumsy lad into a man of fashion. His antechamber crowded with clients and flatterers, Rakewell holds the centre of the stage, magnificently arrayed in velvet cap and silk dressing-gown, yet still lacking the ease of the real dandy. In the person of the hangers-on in the room, Hogarth satirized the aberrations of taste and sportsmanship of his day. The man of

39

11 *Surrounded by Artists and Professors*

fashion must be a connoisseur, and the 'dealers in dark pictures' had furnished him with the *Judgement of Paris*, which hangs incongruously between two pictures of fighting cocks. A heavily-bewigged foreign musician is turning over the pages of a new Italian opera; over the back of his chair a long scroll extending to the floor lists the rich presents offered by the English nobility to Signor Farinelli, the famous Italian *castrato* singer. As a horn-player tunes his instrument noisily, a French dancing-master capers gaily on the Rake's right. Rakewell is being presented with plans for his gardens by Charles Bridgman, principal gardener to the King, who had laid out the palace gardens of Kensington with its Serpentine. His style was severe: formal beds and parterres with

straight vistas of water and regular alleys of trees in contrast to the more romantic and irregular form of landscape gardening instigated by 'Capability' Brown with sudden changes of scene, the whole ornamented with cascades, temples and groves. As a man of fashion, the Rake must also be a sportsman, he must have his cocks at Newmarket and his racers at Epsom, where his horse 'Silly Tom' has just won a cup. Last but not least, he must be prepared for the hazards of London life. Dubois, the famous French duellist (who had been killed in a duel by an Irishman in 1734), instructs him in fencing, and the English prize-fighter champion James Figg, carrying two staves, teaches him the noble art of self-defence. Should these attainments fail to save his skin, he may

40

III *The Tavern Scene*

require the services of the bully, looking fiercely under his cocked hat as he offers his services as bodyguard on the recommendation of 'William Stab.' In the room beyond the archway thronged with tailors and milliners, an old poet in a shabby wig reads his 'Epistle to the Rake.'

Our dandy, however, finds himself more at home in the delights of Covent Garden brothels than in fine society. Having fought and defeated a watchman, whose staff and lantern he has kept as trophies, he has repaired to the Rose Tavern, where he is surrounded by women of the town. The Rose, in Russell Street and Brydges Street, Covent Garden, was a fairly respectable place by day, but late at night was the resort of the worst characters, male and female, and the scene of drunken brawls

and midnight orgies. In this scene, a woman ferociously spurts brandy into the eye of another, who threatens to retaliate with a knife, while a third sets the world on fire—on a map. The Rake, drunk, dishevelled, and exhausted, is being robbed of his watch by a young harlot, who deftly passes it to an accomplice. An entertainment is about to begin: musicians recruited from the street have entered, and the posture woman starts to undress, as Leather-Coat, the master of ceremonies, brings the pewter dish on which she is to perform. This Leather-Coat had made a great reputation for himself as a strong-ribbed man, who, for a pot of beer, would lie down in the street and allow a carriage to pass over him. The room, comfortable as London taverns were, is decorated with

41

IV *Arrested for Debt*

busts of the Caesars, and near the mirror, a portrait bearing the name 'Pontac.' Pontack's, in Abchurch Lane, was a very famous French eating-house, supposedly named after a French Bordeaux magistrate, whose vineyards produced very fine claret.

The next scene presents a magnificent view of St James's Street, the heart of 'High Life' in London, with the gate and towers of St James's Palace closing the vista. On the left in the background, hangs the signboard of White's chocolate house, an exclusive establishment patronized by such wits as Lord Chesterfield, where young men were fleeced and corrupted by fashionable gamblers and profligates. Swift wrote that Robert Harley, 1st Earl of Oxford, 'never passed by White's Choco-

late house (the common rendezvous of infamous sharpers and noble cullies) without bestowing a curse upon that famous academy as the bane of half the English nobility.' It is 1 March, Queen Caroline's birthday, which was also St David's Day, as indicated by the irascible-looking Welshman wearing an enormous leek in his hat, and the street is crowded with coaches and sedan chairs jostling each other on the way to the palace for the birthday celebrations. In an endeavour to retrieve his damaged fortune, the Rake is going to court to solicit a place, but is suddenly stopped by two bailiffs and arrested for debt. Only the intervention of the faithful Sarah Young, now a milliner, saves him from prison.

To replenish his empty purse, Rakewell

v *Marries an Old Maid*

marries an old but wealthy heiress. The ceremony takes place in old Marylebone Church, then on the outskirts of London and much used for private marriages. The bride, toothless and one-eyed, looks tremendously exultant. The bridegroom, now a handsome, portly man, casts sidelong glances at her good-looking lady's maid. His former mistress, accompanied by their child and her mother, tries to force an entrance to stop the ceremony, but is turned back by a vicious-looking pew-opener. Everything in the tumble-down edifice shows signs of decay: the Creed has been destroyed by damp, a crack runs through the commandments, the poor box is covered in cobwebs. In parody of this ill-assorted match, Hogarth placed his dog Trump in one corner paying addresses to a one-eyed lady dog.

From then on, the Rake's career progresses at headlong speed. He has just lost all his newly-acquired wealth in a gaming-house, and in a frenzy of rage and despair, calls down divine retribution upon his own head. A highwayman, with a pistol and black mask in the skirt-pocket of his coat, is so deep lost in melancholy reflections that the little boy bringing him a glass of wine has to tug at his sleeve to attract his attention. An unfortunate parson wrenches his hat down over his face to hide his shame and despair. A nobleman gives his note to a usurer, while the portly gentleman, seated at the table, coolly collects his winnings. So absorbed are losers and winners in their own thoughts, that they fail to notice the flames seen bursting from

43

vi *Scene in a Gaming House*

the wainscot—an allusion to the burning of White's in 1733. Gambling was the prevailing vice of the English aristocracy, and Hogarth portrayed in this scene one of the most notorious court gamblers, Lord William Manners, a brother of the Duke of Rutland. His case was interesting, for whereas gambling ruined most noblemen, Manners made a large private fortune as a professional gamester.

Rakewell has at length been taken to the Fleet, a sinister prison where insolvent debtors were incarcerated, with the filthy, stinking Fleet river running alongside it. At the head of the prison was the warden, a patent office, often let by the holder of the patent to any person who would farm the prison at the highest rate. In 1729, when the Gaol Committee made its cele-

brated inquiry into the state of prisons, the Fleet patent had been held by a certain Huggins who let it out to the infamous Thomas Bambridge. Under the wardenship of Bambridge exorbitant fees were demanded of every prisoner, and men committed for not being able to pay their debts were monstrously ill-treated for not paying fees. More humane conditions prevailed after the removal of Bambridge, but prisoners had still to bring or hire bedding or else sleep on the floor, and (as in Hogarth's print) were pestered by turnkeys for prison fees or garnish moneys; since gaolers received no regular salaries, they had to resort to extracting such fees as they could.

In a final attempt to mend his broken fortunes, Rakewell has tried his hand at

44

VII *Prison Scene*

play-writing, but the curt reply of Manager Rich returning his manuscript, 'Sr. I have read your Play & find it will not doe,' dashed his last hopes. The boy bringing him a pot of beer he has ordered will not leave it except on immediate payment. In an agony of despair, he falls into a swoon. His two fellow prisoners have ruined themselves, one on the left by hare-brained schemes for paying off the national debt, and the other, at the back of the room, by an indefatigable search after the philosopher's stone.

An incurable and dangerous maniac, the Rake is incarcerated in Bethlehem Hospital in Moorfields—Bedlam, and is being manacled before the weeping Sarah. Other inmates include a religious enthusiast in the adjacent cell, an astronomer, a crazy

tailor, and a musician. On the stairs sits the figure of William Ellis, who was believed to have gone mad as a result of his passion for 'charming Betty Careless,' a young harlot renowned for the innocence of her countenance and the lewdness of her ways, whose name he has written on the hand rail. A crazy theorist draws on the walls plans to discover longitude by the firing of bombs—a shaft at William Whiston, an eccentric country clergyman and physicist protected by Queen Caroline. A 'Pope' is saying mass. The wooden basin on the floor contains gruel, the normal food of prisoners. A lady of fashion, carrying a fan, and her attendant survey the scene, for Bedlam in the eighteenth century was a popular resort for Londoners. The hospital, a noble building with man-

45

VIII *Scene in a Madhouse*

sarded roof, finished in 1676 to the design of Robert Hooke, was adorned at the entrance with 'admirable statues' depicting 'Melancholy' and 'Raving Madness,' and surrounded with spacious walks. Visitors paid for admittance to marvel at the strange humours of the patients. This custom increased the hospital's income, and not till 1770 did it occur to the authorities that the constant stream of onlookers 'tended to disturb the tranquillity of the patients'. The hospital had room for 200 lunatics, each with a cell to himself in which he or she was locked up at night;

most had beds but raving cases, who were manacled, slept on straw. Patients were admitted every Saturday when they were examined by the Committee and the resident Physician, and if 'judged a fit object' a warrant of admittance was drawn up by the President. Relatives or other persons bringing a patient had to guarantee to take him away when discharged or to bury him when dead. On stifling summer nights Bedlam became a scene of horror as the cries of the lunatics, tortured by the heat, and the rattle of their chains echoed across Moorfields.

INDUSTRY AND
IDLENESS

INDUSTRY AND IDLENESS: 'Designed & Engrav'd by W^m. Hogarth. Publish'd according to Act of Parliament 30 Sep. 1747.'

Announced in The General Advertiser *for 17 October 1747 :* 'This Day is publish'd, Price 12s. *Design'd and Engrav'd by MR HOGARTH. Twelve Prints call'd INDUSTRY AND IDLENESS, Shewing the Advantages attending the former, and the miserable effects of the latter, in the different Fortunes of Two Apprentices. To be had at the Golden Head in Leicester-Fields, and at the Print-shops.'*

1 *The Fellow 'Prentices at their Looms*

EIGHTEENTH-CENTURY moralists in general paid little attention to the subtleties of human nature, and drew the clearest-cut contrast between good and evil. This is certainly the case with *Industry and Idleness*, the most ambitious series Hogarth undertook, and a study in the contrasted careers of two Spitalfields apprentices: Frank Goodchild and Tom Idle, the former wholly virtuous and the latter wholly wicked. Thackeray expressed sympathy with Tom Idle, whom he thought never had a chance in life, and the modern psychologist would probably agree. On the other hand, the series is invaluable as a picture of life in eighteenth-century London and packed with contemporary detail. In it we see a picture of the City at its zenith. The Corporation of London was the most dignified, the most powerful of all municipal bodies.

Practically a state within a state, with its chief magistrate, Court of Aldermen and Common Council, analogous to the King, Lords and Commons of the Realm, it was policed, in so far as it was policed at all, by its own constables and guarded by its own militia. The City was less amenable to the jurisdiction of court and Parliament than any other portion of English soil, and was rendered more formidable to the government by the presence within its precincts of the largest and least manageable mob in England. The great merchant princes of the City were almost as closely intermarried as the aristocracy, and so influential that the Elder Pitt planned his military campaigns in consultation with them.

In the government of the City, the Livery Companies played a crucial part, since freedom of the City was reserved to their members. The Livery Companies des-

49

11 *The Industrious 'Prentice performing the Duty of a Christian*

cended from the merchant guilds which flourished in the thirteenth and fourteenth centuries. As the population of London had increased and trades become more numerous, citizens had begun to associate in distinct companies, according to their respective occupations, and to seek charters of incorporation and protection for the purpose of excluding non-freemen from exercising the same trade within the precincts of the City. Each company had its master, wardens, assistants and clerks for the general management of its affairs. There were seventy-eight companies, including the Twelve Great Livery Companies, so-called because of their superior wealth and prestige: the Mercers, the Grocers, the Drapers, the Fishmongers, the Goldsmiths, the Skinners, the Merchant Taylors, the Haberdashers, the Salters, the Ironmongers, the Vintners and the Cloth-

Workers. The Drapers Company (to which Goodchild would have belonged) had in proportion produced more Lord Mayors than any other company; indeed the first Lord Mayor of London (1189-1212), Henry Fitz-Alwyn, belonged to the fraternity of drapers.

The Corporation of the City of London consisted of three separate chambers: the Court of Common Hall, the Court of Aldermen, and the Court of Common Council. Liverymen of the respective City Companies, which constituted the Common Hall, annually elected the Lord Mayor and two sheriffs of London.

The Court of Aldermen, composed of twenty-five aldermen sitting under the Lord Mayor, formed the executive part of the City's government. Aldermen were elected by the freemen of each of the City's twenty-five wards (for life), subject

III *The Idle 'Prentice at Play in the Church Yard during Divine Service*

only to the approval of their own court as 'fit and proper persons,' but were otherwise irremovable and to that extent irresponsible. Each alderman had the direction of affairs in his ward under the general supervision of the Lord Mayor. In 1741 George II by letters patent empowered all Aldermen of London without distinction to act as justices of the peace within the City.

The Court of the Common Council, consisting of the Lord Mayor, the Aldermen and Common Councilmen, elected annually by the freemen of each ward, formed the legislature. Assembling in the Guildhall whenever summoned by the Lord Mayor, it made bye-laws for the good government of the City, and controlled most of the vast amount of property owned by the Corporation.

In the series Hogarth presents a rather idealized picture of the apprenticeship system, which had fallen short of the genuine educational purposes which its Elizabethan and early Stuart promoters had intended, and was often used by unscrupulous masters as a means of obtaining cheap labour. On the other hand, it was still possible for the industrious apprentice to become a master in his turn, or else an apprentice could obtain his freedom by exemption or fine. According to the terms of the indenture or contract between master and apprentice, the master had to feed, clothe, and house his apprentice for seven years or more, and in return could exact an unlimited number of hours of work. He had in actual fact difficulty in doing so, for apprentices, in London especially, were traditionally idle and often turbulent; they roamed the streets, often engaging in pitched battles with apprentices of neigh-

51

IV *The Industrious 'Prentice a Favourite, and entrusted by his Master*

bouring parishes, and often associated
with prostitutes who tempted them to rob
their masters. Hogarth, however, made his
apprentices Spitalfields weavers, who were
regarded as a type of the highly intelligent
and skilled craftsmen who flourished under
the domestic system. In the seventeenth
century French Huguenot refugees had
founded the silk-weaving industry of
Spitalfields and its weavers had soon
become world-famous. Manufacturers in
such trades were still in close touch with
their workmen, maintaining a strong pat-
riarchal attitude towards them, and dis-
ciplining them like children. Weavers'
houses generally consisted of two rooms on
the ground floor and a workroom above,
with a large window to let light on to the
looms. In small, crowded, often dirty surroundings, working from twelve to sixteen hours a day, some of the most delicate

and exquisitely wrought brocades, satins,
and black velvets were produced, and also
tapestries and hangings for houses.

The first scene shows us the interior of a
weaver's workshop, with two apprentices
at their looms. The looms were to some
extent antiquated since they did not incor-
porate the fly shuttle which had been invented by John Kay in 1733, and which
enormously increased the speed of weav-
ing. On the right, Goodchild, plump and
bright-featured, is working diligently, his
'Prentice Guide' carefully open beside
him. It was the custom for apprentices to
weavers to sing at their looms, and behind
him several ballads are pinned to the wall,
including 'Whitington, Ld. Mayor' and
'The London Prentice.' On the left, Tom
Idle, dirty and unkempt, snores with his
mouth open, having drunk the half gallon
pot of beer before him. A kitten plays with

v *The Idle 'Prentice turn'd away and Sent to Sea*

his shuttle, on the floor his book of instructions lies in tatters, and his unused spinning wheel bears no flax; on his loom he has hung the ballad 'Moll Flanders' showing in which direction his interests lie. The door of the room is suddenly opened by the master, who calls out to the sleeper, and threatens him with his stick.

It is Sunday morning, inside a church, probably St Martin-in-the-Fields. Goodchild, wearing a long-skirted coat, shares a hymn-book with his master's daughter, a comely young woman, wearing a smart cap trimmed with ribbons. An immensely fat woman, whose expression denotes a high sense of her own self-importance, shares their pew; behind Goodchild is a man asleep. A prominent figure is the elderly pew-opener on the left, with a bunch of keys at her waist, turned away from the body of the church, so as to spy new arrivals. The preacher is about to begin his sermon; the fat reader and lean clerk in their respective desks below the pulpit and the small figures in the gallery display wealth of characterization, although unfortunately on so reduced a scale as to be somewhat out of perspective. An interesting detail is the row of three-cornered hats or beavers, hanging on hooks in front of the gallery on the left. The middle aisle of the church, where seats were free, is considerably more crowded than the pews, several of which are empty.

Meanwhile, the worthless Idle is in a churchyard, gambling on a tombstone with three pickpockets of approximately his own age. The game is that of hustlecap and the wicked apprentice tries to cheat by hiding some of the halfpence under the broad brim of his hat, much to the indignation of a shoeblack and a sinis-

53

VI *The Industrious 'Prentice out of his Time, and married to his Master's Daughter*

ter fellow with a patch over his eye. In the words of Hogarth's biographer, Austin Dobson, 'there is no more eloquent stroke in the whole of Hogarth than that by which the miserable player at "halfpenny under the hat" in Plate 3, is shown to have but a plank between him and the grave.' The group is so engrossed in the game as to be unaware of the irate churchwarden alarmingly brandishing a cane.

The industrious apprentice has been transferred to the office, and his master, Mr West, in Quaker's dress, is seen leaning affectionately upon his shoulder. Goodchild stands at an escritoire from which he has just taken a ledger, and holds a bunch of keys in his right hand and a money bag in his left hand. The pair of gloves clasping hands indicates that a partnership is about to take place. A red-nosed porter, wearing a shield round his neck with the arms of the City of London, is delivering rolls of cloth from Blackwell Hall.

The idle apprentice, having tired the patience of his master, is shipped off to sea (it was the custom for young offenders and vagrants to be sent to sea). As he is ferried to a waiting ship, accompanied by his elderly mother, wearing a widow's coif, he defiantly tosses his indenture into the water. A sailor with a sinister countenance is rowing; a waterman significantly points to a gibbet from which hangs an executed pirate, while the other boy shows him a cat-o'-nine-tails, a symbol of the discipline awaiting him on board the ship. Idle replies by a rude gesture, pointing at Cuckhold's Point, which they have just passed, a reach of the Thames opposite West India docks between Limehouse and Greenwich.

The good apprentice, now a partner in the firm, as the sign 'West and Goodchild' shows, is further rewarded for his good conduct by marrying his master's daughter.

54

VII *The Idle 'Prentice return'd from Sea, and in a Garret with a common Prostitute*

Goodchild and his wife, in night attire, are drinking tea—a sign of affluence—by the open window. He is handing money to the leader of a kettledrum band, which has been giving them the customary wedding serenade. Butchers often performed this function, and Hogarth introduced two of them playing on a cleaver with a bone. It was also the custom in the eighteenth century to give away the remnants of the wedding banquet to the poor, and accordingly a kneeling woman is collecting victuals which a footman is pouring into her apron. The legless beggar in the picture, holding the broadside of a ballad 'Jesse or the Happy Pair,' was a man known as Philip the Tub, a regular attendant at weddings. The street is situated near the Monument, designed by Sir Christopher Wren, the pedestal of which appears in the distance, bearing the inscription: 'In remembrance —of Burning the Protestant City by the treachery of the Papist Faction in—year —of Our—Lo—d 1666.'

Returned from the sea after a long voyage, Tom Idle has become a footpad. The door of his den is strongly bolted and barred, so as to make his retreat secure. Seen here in a state of acute panic, he has just been awakened by the noise of a cat dropping down the chimney in pursuit of a rat, dislodging some bricks on its way. His companion, a low prostitute, appears to be completely unperturbed, as she admires an ear-ring; in her lap lie two watches and chains, the total of last night's plunder. The frightful state of the garret, the broken-down bed, the damp plaster dropping off the walls and ceiling, and every sign of disrepair, probably gives a fair picture of the conditions in which poor people lived at the time.

The next scene is set in Old Fishmongers' Company Hall, built by Edward

7

8

VIII *The Industrious 'Prentice Grown Rich, and Sheriff of London*

Jerman, the City Surveyor, after the Great Fire. The gastronomic activities of the City notables were notorious (Fishmongers' dinners being among the most famous of City banquets), and guzzling of gargantuan proportions is in progress. In a gallery over two of the windows a band of musicians are performing. Grown rich, Goodchild has become Sheriff of London, a step towards the office of Lord Mayor, and is seen here with his wife in the principal seats, with the sword and mace at their sides. An imposing beadle with his state gown, holding a long staff, stands at the entrance door as a messenger delivers an address to Goodchild. The print is of great interest as regards table manners in the eighteenth century, when all dishes were placed on the table at once but no wine, the latter being handed round by a waiter. The company would later retire to the

gardens, at the back of the hall, for dessert.

Next, we follow Idle into the sinister Bloody Bowl cellar, a resort of thieves and prostitutes, situated in Alsatia, the criminal district between the Thames and Fleet Street. A notorious place of refuge for persons wishing to avoid bailiffs and creditors, and felons generally, it took its name from the Landgraviate of Alsace, in Latin Alsatia, familiar to England's Low Country soldiers as a borderland, a seat of contention. With its impenetrable network of courts and alleys, it was, wrote Fielding, 'a vast wood or forest in which the thief may harbour with as great security as wild beasts do in the deserts of Arabia and Africa.' Night-cellars, which abounded in the district, offered drink and shelter to thieves and other criminals. Idle and his accomplice are in the centre of the cellar, dividing the booty obtained by murder-

9

56

IX *The Idle 'Prentice betrayed by his W — e, and taken in a Night Cellar with his Accomplice*

ing a passer-by, whose body is being thrust through a trap-door built especially for the purpose. A brawl is in progress and Idle, betrayed by his strumpet, is arrested by the High Constable and his men. (He was unlucky; normally for one criminal caught, six escaped.)

The two former apprentices are brought together again in dramatic circumstances. Goodchild, wearing the furred robes and gold chain of an Alderman, sits as a magistrate in the Guildhall (two Aldermen sat in turn to administer justice), when Idle is brought before him on a charge of murder. The clerk is busily writing out a warrant committing to Newgate the quivering prisoner, who crouches in abject supplication. His mother, still in widow's weeds, speaks to a stout beadle, holding his staff of office. Idle's accomplice, the man in the knitted cap and eye-patch, his companion

in the churchyard game and in Bloody Bowl Cellar, has turned King's evidence. In the corner, an official is accepting a bribe from a slatternly woman to allow the accomplice to use his left hand in attesting the oath on the book—it was a common superstition that an oath taken in this fashion was not binding.

Found guilty, Idle would have waited in Newgate, where the bellman of the Church of St Sepulchre would visit him at midnight on the eve of his execution, awakening him with 'twelve solemn towles with double strokes' of a heavy hand bell, admonishing him and his fellow prisoners in the lugubrious doggerel verse:
All you that in the condemned hole do lie,
Prepare you, for tomorrow you shall die.
Watch all and pray : the hour is drawing near. . .
At daybreak, the great bell of St Sepulchre, 'used only to toll when the prisoners are

57

x *The Industrious 'Prentice Alderman of London, the Idle one brought before him and impeached by his Accomplice*

carried to be executed at Tyburn,' would strike again as the death-cart drew up. The parish clerk would then deliver a pious exhortation, urging the bystanders to repent of their wickedness and pray for the condemned sinners. Nosegays would be thrust into the felons' hands and they would proceed on their journey to Tyburn. Tyburn had been a place of execution since the twelfth century, and there the gallows, or Triple Tree, standing on three legs, was erected permanently, in an open space at the end of the present Edgware Road, near where Marble Arch now stands. Hogarth's print is the best view of Tyburn in existence. The prisoner is standing in an open tumbril in front of his coffin, receiving spiritual solace from a Wesleyan preacher (he holds a book marked Westleys), as the hangman adjusts the rope on one of the beams. The artist in

this print is concerned, not so much with the fate of one man, as in giving a humorous representation of an execution holiday, or Tyburn Fair, as it was called, which was often the pretext for general uproar and even riots. Tyburn Fair provided an education in brutality, in a world where the gallows, exploits of felons and executions figured largely in the press and current literature of the day. It attracted enormous crowds, and Fielding wrote indignantly of the 'barbarous custom peculiar to the English of insulting and jesting at misery.' Around the gibbet were erected open galleries like a race-course stand, wherein seats were let to spectators at executions. The key of one of them was kept by Mother Douglas, a procuress who kept a brothel in Covent Garden, and who was nicknamed for that reason 'the Tyburn pew-opener.' Hogarth pictures

58

XI *The Idle 'Prentice executed at Tyburn*

her here in a grandstand, drinking gin with her associates, and raising her hand in sanctimonious horror; a soldier helps a girl into the same cart. Beside them, also in a cart, stands Idle's mother, crying. The cake-seller on the right, dressed like a person of quality, was 'Tiddy Doll', so known because he always sang the end of the ballad with that title. The king of itinerant tradesmen, he was invariably present on such occasions. A boy has overturned a wheelbarrow full of apples, which was being pushed by a girl; she retaliates by striking him in the face. A man brandishes a small dog, preparing to throw it at Idle, while a kneeling soldier picks a man's pocket. A ragged woman cries the dying speech of Thomas Idle—printed the day before his execution. In the distance, we can see the green slopes of Notting Hill.

In the last episode, Francis Goodchild reaches the summit of his worldly ambition by becoming Lord Mayor of London. On the 9th of November the new Lord Mayor would be met at the Guildhall by the Aldermen, Recorder and Sheriffs of London, would embark on the City barge and proceed by water to Westminster with much pageantry, to take the oath. He would return in the same manner to Black Friars stairs, whence the livery of the City Companies had marched to their stands, preceded by flying colours and bands of music. At length he would proceed to the Guildhall for the inauguration dinner, which consisted principally of a baron of beef (weighing three hundredweight) brought in procession from the kitchen, placed on a pedestal and cut up by the 'City Carver.' The next morning, remains of the banquet were doled out to the poor.

Goodchild is shown riding pompously in a gilded carriage, in richly furred scarlet robes with velvet hood and gold chain, accompanied by Mr Swordbearer in a cap like a reversed saucepan, which this great officer wore on such occasions. The print contains a brilliant representation of the west end of Cheapside; looking southwards across St Paul's churchyard we see the eastern end of the cathedral, while in front, a balcony projects from the first

59

XII *The Industrious 'Prentice Lord-Mayor of London*

floor of a house at the corner of Paternoster Row. In the balcony, several personages, including the egregious Frederick, Prince of Wales, and his wife, the Princess Augusta, stand under a canopy of state. According to Horace Walpole, the person on the extreme right was the Countess of Middlesex, Mistress of the Robes. The usual place for royalty to see the Show was at Bow Church, but on one occasion Frederick wishing to see it privately entered the City in disguise. He was discovered by some members of the Saddlers' Company, and asked to occupy the Company's stand. He accepted the invitation, and soon after became a Saddler.

Hogarth's print contains a wealth of comic characters and incidents, including the oversetting of a stand opposite on which some girls were standing. In the right-hand corner, an emaciated boy, a hawker of broadsides, holds a paper on which is printed 'A full and true account of the ghost of Tho. Idle.' The company of journeymen butchers, with their marrowbones and cleavers, are the most noisy if not the most enthusiastic section of the crowd. The artist reserved his chief ridicule for the City militia, or volunteers, a motley group of undisciplined men of all ages, sizes and heights, so unused to muskets as not to know how to hold them.

60

MARRIAGE
À LA MODE

MARRIAGE À LA MODE: 'Engraved by G. Scotin, B. Baron and S. Ravenet. Invented Painted & Published by W^m. Hogarth According to Act of Parliament April 1st 1745.'

Advertised in The London Daily Post *for 2 April 1743: 'MR HOGARTH intends to publish by Subscription* SIX PRINTS *from Copper-Plates, engrav'd by the best Masters in Paris, after his own Paintings (the Heads, for the better Preservation of the Characters and Expressions, to be done by the Author); representing a Variety of* Modern Occurrences in High Life, *and called MARRIAGE À LA MODE. Particular care is taken that the whole Work shall not be liable to Exception on Account of any Indecency or Inelegancy, and that none of the Characters represented shall be personal. N.B. The Subscription will be One Guinea; Half to be paid on Subscribing, and the other half on the delivery of the Prints, which will be with all possible speed, the Author being determin'd to engage in no other work till this is compleated. The Price will be one Guinea and an Half, after the Subscription is over, and no Copies will be made of them. Subscriptions are taken in at Mr Hogarth's, the Golden Head in Leicester Fields; where may be had all his engrav'd Works.'*

1 *The Contract*

1. MARRIAGE À LA MODE, in which Hogarth paints fashionable Georgian society, is the most skilfully drawn and most imaginative of his picture dramas. It is subtler than his other series, for in it the downfall of his hero and heroine is caused not by the force of outside circumstances, but by the inherent conflict of their own passions and weaknesses.

The hero is an earl's son, idle, supercilious and dissipated, the heroine, the spoilt child of a rich merchant, and their story begins with the signing of the marriage contract, which took place immediately before the church ceremony. In a magnificent drawing-room, profusely adorned with Old Masters, the bridegroom's father, an old earl, impoverished

and racked with gout, sits proudly holding his pedigree. Through the open window, we see his sumptuous Palladian residence, perhaps designed by William Kent or Lord Burlington himself, work on which is now interrupted through lack of funds. The bride's father, an Alderman of London, and a shrewd man of business, refusing to be impressed, scrutinizes the financial provisions of the marriage settlement. The earl's steward, standing at the table holding two bank-notes, shows his master a mortgage deed, as if to mollify him. Viscount Squanderfield, the bridegroom, an effeminate fop, takes snuff and is too absorbed in the contemplation of his own finery in the mirror to look at his future wife, who, wearing a bridal dress of white satin, plays with the engagement ring she

63

II *The Breakfast Scene*

has threaded on her handkerchief, and receives the pronounced attentions of Counsellor Silvertongue, a sleek young lawyer.

The next episode shows the newly-wed pair at breakfast; it is early afternoon, yet lights are still smouldering in the heavy chandeliers. After an all-night card-party, the lady of the house stretches and yawns, capricious, idle and voluptuous. She casts a contemptuous sidelong glance at her husband, who sags dejectedly in his chair, worn out and nauseated after an independent nocturnal expedition. A little dog sniffs inquisitively at the woman's cap stuffed in his pocket. Neither of them is in the mood for business, and the faithful Methodist steward, carrying a sheaf of unpaid bills and only one receipt, has been ordered to come back another day. Beyond

the marble pillars in the adjoining room, a yawning footman languidly arranges the furniture. The room is said to have been copied from the drawing-room of Horace Walpole's house in Arlington Street.

The young nobleman has not only dissipated his wife's fortune, he has also injured his health, and in the next scene we see him visiting a French quack, 'Mon^r de la Pillule,' for treatment of a venereal disease. He holds out a box of ineffectual pills, flourishing his stick at the sneering quack. The cause of the evil, a sad little girl dressed in adult finery, is a pathetic figure; Hazlitt wrote of her: 'nothing can be more striking than the contrast between the extreme softness of her person and the hardened indifference of her character. The vacant stillness, the docility to vice,

III *The Scene with the Quack*

the premature suppression of youthful sensibility, the doll-like mechanism of the whole figure, which seems to have no other feeling but a sickly sense of pain—shows the deepest insight into human nature.' The consulting room is decorated with skulls, and all the paraphernalia of the quack; as in Garth's 'Dispensary'

Here mummies lie, most reverently stale,
And there, the tortoise hung her coat of mail:
Not far from some huge shark's devouring head,
The flying fish their finny pinions spread;
Aloft, in rows, large poppy-heads were strung,
And near, a scaly alligator hung;
In this place, drugs in musty heaps decay'd,
In that, dry'd bladders and drawn teeth were laid.

The quack (as is explained in the title-page of the open book bearing his name as author) is also the inventor of the complicated machine we see on the floor, which is designed for re-setting collar-bones and also, if need be, for opening bottles.

From the gloomy consulting-room, we pass to the bedroom of the heroine—now a countess. She has just returned from an auction of fashionable *objets d'art*, such as the figurines and other knick-knacks strewn on the floor, and is now at her *toilette*. Two foreign performers, a wooden-featured German flute-player called Weidemann, and a bloated bejewelled Italian, Giovanni Carestini, a *castrato* singer, are introduced—savage caricatures giving vent to Hogarth's spleen against foreign artists. Carestini's voice was described by a contemporary as 'at first a powerful and clear

4.

65

IV *The Toilette Scene*

soprano, which afterwards changed into the fullest, finest and deepest counter-tenor that has perhaps ever been heard.' The lady in the straw hat, rocking herself to the notes in ecstasy, was Mrs Fox-Lane, later Lady Bingley, notorious for her passion for Italian music, whose blasphemous cry, 'One God, one Farinelli,' had electrified the opera house. Farinelli, who was reputed to have had the 'finest voice in the world,' was principal chorister in the Pope's chapel in Rome; he had come to England in 1734, was introduced to the King, and sang before the whole royal family. The lady's fat husband, whip in hand, has been lulled to sleep. A lean dandy in curl-papers with a vacant countenance—said to have represented Herr Michel, the Prussian envoy—sips choco-late contentedly. The hostess, now a mother (a child's comforter hangs at the back of her chair), is having her hair dressed by a Swiss barber. Silvertongue, reclining on a sofa, with the easy familiarity of a privileged visitor, points to a representation of a masquerade on the screen, and, flourishing tickets in his hand, persuades her to attend one. Masquerades had first been introduced into England from Italy in the sixteenth century, and given new vogue at the beginning of the eighteenth century by the Swiss, Heidegger. Denounced by Fielding as 'the temples of drunkenness, lewdness, and all kinds of debauchery,' they were popular, he added, since 'pleasure always hath been and always will be the principal business of persons of fashion and fortune . . . to

66

v *The Death of the Earl*

the upper part of mankind time is an enemy, and . . . their chief labour is to kill it.'

After the masquerade, Silvertongue succeeded in persuading the countess to spend the night with him at the Turk's Head, a Covent Garden bagnio. Originally bathing establishments, bagnios had become places of assignation, where rooms were rented to any couple from five shillings to half a guinea a night. A dying fire lights the hastily discarded clothes of the lovers in the dingy room. Surprised by the earl, who forced an entrance seeking to avenge his honour, Silvertongue has transfixed him and as he collapses, his guilty wife frantically entreats his pardon. Alarmed by the noise, a lean old man, the keeper of the place, has summoned a watchman and a constable, whose hand holds a lantern, but Silvertongue makes a precipitate retreat through the window into the darkness.

The unhappy countess has now returned to the sordid home of her parsimonious father. The bare room is decorated with coarse, unfashionable Dutch paintings, and through the open casement we see a view of old London Bridge crowded with tottering houses. London Bridge was the first and, until the opening of Westminster Bridge in 1750, the only bridge across the Thames in the metropolis. In Elizabethan times it was adorned with 'sumptuous buildings,' shops and houses, some with platform roofs and charming gardens. In 1666 the labyrinth of then dilapidated buildings was swept away by the Great

67

Fire, but the whole street was rebuilt within twenty years, being twenty feet broad in Hogarth's time. In 1746 the Corporation of London decided, because of the high cost of upkeep, as well as the many accidents caused by fast-driven carriages in the congested street, to clear the bridge of all buildings, and in 1757 its houses were demolished and it was surrounded by parapets and balustrades.

In these depressing surroundings, taunted with the bitter reproaches of her father, the countess in despair has bribed a servant to procure poison for her. The smug physician, vexed at her dying before taking his medicament, takes the half-witted footboy to task, sternly pointing to the empty bottle labelled 'laudanum' on the floor. Counsellor Silvertongue has hung at Tyburn for murder (his 'Last Dying Speech' lies at his dead mistress's feet). Her father, while pretending to feel her pulse, is in fact callously removing a valuable ring from his daughter's finger before *rigor* sets in. The only sign of real sorrow comes from the old nurse, who lifts up the crippled child with its heavy leg-iron to kiss the mother. It is a girl, and so the title is now extinct. 'Such are the Dead Sea fruit of the Marriage à la Mode.'

INDIVIDUAL
ENGRAVINGS

SOUTHWARK FAIR: Invented Painted and Engrav^d by Wm Hogarth. 1733. [1735 See A Rake's Progress.]

THE LAUGHING AUDIENCE: (W. Hogarth) (1733). Subscription Ticket to A Rake's Progress *and* Southwark Fair.

THE SLEEPING CONGREGATION: 'Invented Engraved & Published October 26 1736 by Wm Hogarth Pursuant to an Act of Parliament. Price one Shilling.'

STROLLING ACTRESSES DRESSING IN A BARN: 'Invented, Painted, Engraved & Published, by W^m. Hogarth, March 25 1738. According to Act of Parliament.' *See* The Four Times of the Day.

THE MARCH TO FINCHLEY: 'A Representation of the March of the Guards towards Scotland, in the year 1745.
'Painted by Willm. Hogarth & Publish'd Decbr. 1750. According to Act of Parliament. Engrav'd by Luke Sullivan.'
Announced in The General Advertiser *for 16 March, 1750:* 'MR HOGARTH proposes to publish by SUBSCRIPTION, *a Print representing the March to* FINCHLEY *in the Year 1746, engraved on a Copper-Plate 22 inches by 17, Price 7s. 6d. Subscriptions may be taken at his House the Golden-Head in Leicester-Fields, till the 30th of April next; during which Time, the Picture may be seen and not longer, to the End that the Engraving may not be retarded.* Note, *Each Print will be Half a Guinea after the Subscription is over.*'
Hogarth had intended to dedicate the print to George II. The king, however, dearly loved military discipline, and on being shown it exclaimed indignantly 'What a bainter *burlesque a soldier? he deserves to be picketed for his insolence! Take his trumpery out of my sight'; much mortified, the artist dedicated it to Frederick the Great instead.*

BEER STREET: 'Design'd by W. Hogarth. Publish'd according to Act of Parliament Feb. 1, 1751. Price 1s.'

GIN LANE: 'Design'd by W. Hogarth. Publish'd according to Act of Parliam^t Feb. 1 1751. Price 1s.' *Verses to appear below the design were composed by Hogarth's friend, the Rev. James Townley.*

THE INVASION—ENGLAND: 'Design'd and Etch'd by W^m. Hogarth. Publish'd according to Act of Parliament March 8th, 1756.' *David Garrick posed for the picture of the eager young recruit, and wrote the verses accompanying the print.*

THE COCKPIT: 'Design'd and Engrav'd by Willm Hogarth. Publish'd according to Act of Parliament Nov. 5 1759.'
Advertised in The London Chronicle *for Dec. 1-4 1759:* 'This Day was published, Price 3s. A PRINT; *designed and engraved by* MR. HOGARTH, *representing a* COCK-MATCH.'

THE STAGE COACH; OR, COUNTRY INN YARD: 'Price one shilling. Design'd and Engrav'd by W. Hogarth.—Publish'd According to Act of Parliament. 1747.'

Southwark Fair

SOUTHWARK FAIR, which had been in existence since the sixteenth century, was held on St Margaret's Hill in early September and usually lasted fourteen days. Formally opened by the Lord Mayor in procession, it was the resort of 'persons of all distinctions of both sexes,' and though often the scene of disorders, was not suppressed until 1762.

Hogarth shows the fairground in the distance, and the whole foreground crowded with performers and spectators, as tragedians and comedians posture and rant beneath banners and painted sign-boards advertising their repertoire. On the left, the performance of 'The Fall of Bajazet' is rudely interrupted by the collapse of the temporary stage. The woman in the china booth below hastily endeavours to escape being crushed to death. On the right, waxworks depict the whole court of France—a well-known exhibition of the period. Violante, a noted rope-dancer, swings gracefully above the heads of the spectators, and descending by means of a rope from the church tower is Cadman, 'the famed Icarus of the rope.' The bald-headed man on a pony is the great James Figg, known as the 'Atlas of the Sword,' who kept a booth at the Fair, advertising himself as the 'Master of the Noble Science of Defence.' The focus of the whole design is the handsome girl beating a drum followed by many admirers. Hogarth, passing through the fair on a previous occasion, had seen the master of the company strike the fair drummer; he at once intervened, and gave the brute a sound drubbing.

The Laughing Audience

THE eighteenth century was not a great age for the theatre. Under Sir Robert Walpole, a certain life was still to be found on the stage because it was a battle-ground for politics, with such vigorous productions as Gay's *Beggar's Opera*. Later, however, partly because of the tightening of licensing laws, eighteenth-century drama reached its nadir with a succession of turgid, conventional plays, and bowdlerized versions of Shakespeare, including *King Lear* with a happy ending! The situation was to some extent redeemed by the dramatic genius of Hogarth's friend, David Garrick, but not till some decades later, with the advent of Sheridan and Goldsmith, was there any real improvement. Built up from the sketches of men and women in Hogarth's notebooks, the engraving shows the occupants of the pit convulsed with laughter, in contrast to the more fashionable personages in the boxes, who are too engrossed in their personal affairs to pay any attention to the stage. The orchestra is separated from the pit by a barrier with iron spikes designed to restrain over-vigorous demonstrations of disapproval.

The Sleeping Congregation

T HE SLEEPING CONGREGATION shows us an eighteenth-century church service, typical of an age when religious enthusiasm was frowned upon, when rationalized Christianity was the order of the day, and when bishops spent much of their time managing the governmental electoral interest in their diocese. In the pulpit, the droning of the preacher, who has taken as his text Matthew xi, 28, 'Come unto me, all ye that labour . . . and I will give you rest,' has lulled the entire congregation to slumber. Long after the sand has run out in his hourglass, the interminable sermon continues. In the pews men are snoring loudly, and two old women in steeple hats have fallen asleep standing. Only the clerk has managed to stay awake and leers at a well-developed young woman whose prayer-book lies open at the service 'of matrimony.' The preacher was Dr John Theophilus Desaguiliers, who was chaplain to the Prince of Wales.

Strolling Actresses Dressing in a Barn

I N a dilapidated barn, strolling players prepare for a performance. In the centre 'Diana,' a buxom young woman, has just discarded her hoop and petticoat, and is declaiming her part in stockings and chemise. Next to her, 'Flora' dresses her hair with a tallow candle and a flour-dredger, before a large hamper labelled 'Jewels,' while on the other side two small boys dressed as imps refresh themselves from a jug of porter. Actresses in the costumes of a page and a nun are clutching a cat and drawing blood from its tail to lend realism to some sanguinary scene. On the extreme right a 'tragedy queen' with crown and mantle is rehearsing her part as Juno with sublime conviction, majestically stretching out her leg on an overturned wheelbarrow to allow a young woman to darn a hole in her stock-ing. On the left, a girl dressed as an eagle feeds a frightened child. 'Ganymede,' the *jeune premier*, deprived of breeches, takes a glass of gin from a 'Siren,' who wears a large fishtail tied to her waist. On a ladder 'Cupid' reaches out for Apollo's stockings that are hanging out to dry in the 'clouds.' The two play-bills lying on the bed give the key to the characters in the forthcoming entertainment to be played at the George Inn, London. Several tallow candles intended to illuminate the theatre are on the ground. Theatrical properties lie everywhere—a chariot, a dragon, a classical altar and rollers for a stormy sea on which roost chickens expelled from their usual perches; yet the tawdriness of the surroundings is redeemed by the obvious and unquestioning faith of the actors in their art.

The March to Finchley

IN December 1745 the Young Preten-
der reached Derby. Though the news
caused great consternation in London and there was a run on the
Bank of England, there was no panic. It
was announced that the King would go to
an encampment at Finchley, and there-
upon the weavers offered him a thousand
men, and the lawyers formed themselves
into a small army to defend the royal
family. It was this spirit which Hogarth
captured in this print, where he shows the
Footguards, accompanied by militia regi-
ments and a host of volunteers, marching
by the Tottenham Court Turnpike to the
improvised camp set up at Finchley. The
head of the column marches away in the
distance, but the rear-guard has broken
ranks as it approaches the narrow turnpike. Stragglers, drunkards and camp-fol-
lowers form a jostling crowd inextricably
mixed with a pieman, a milkmaid, a chim-
ney-sweep, and (on the left) a pair of
Jacobite spies holding a treasonable letter.
The King's Head on the right is wholly
occupied by inmates from Mother Douglas' Covent Garden brothel, with the pro-
prietress herself, her vast bosom overhang-
ing the window ledge, uttering a patriotic
cry, her eyes lifted up to heaven. In front
of the Adam and Eve opposite, a brawl is
in progress. In the foreground, a tall grenadier is being simultaneously attacked by
his two lady loves, one hawking opposition
newspapers, and the other selling government ballad-sheets. On a cart, beside two
pipe-smoking soldiers' wives, a young
woman of great beauty sits quietly nursing
her baby, with a small boy at her feet
blowing a tin trumpet.

Beer Street

BEER STREET glorifies England's national drink, and shows the prosperity and jollity of eighteenth-century England, where food was plentiful and reasonably cheap. In contrast to *Gin Lane*, which follows, here all is cheerful and thriving. The pawnbroker's is the only house going to ruin, and even the small quantity of porter he can procure is taken in at the wicket, to avoid the importunities of creditors. On the left, a butcher and a blacksmith, waving a shoulder of mutton, are each grasping a foaming tankard. Next to them, a drayman is whispering endearments to a servantmaid, one arm round her neck. The sign-painter was identified as John Stephen Liotard, a fashionable portrait-painter. One of the two fisherwomen seated on the pavement in front of the picture, holds a broadsheet, 'A New Ballad on the Herring Fishery,' by John Lockman, the 'Herring Poet,' secretary of the British White Herring Fishery Company, and a friend of Hogarth.

Gin Lane

GIN LANE was a frontal attack on the national addiction to gin, the cause of so many evils, and Hogarth expressed his moral indignation with great artistic genius. The scene is that part of St Giles' known as the Rookeries, where every fourth house was a gin-shop. Steps lead down to a cellar, over the doorway the sinister inscription:

> *Drunk for a Penny,*
> *Dead drunk for two pence,*
> *Clean straw for nothing.*

The emaciated figure holding an empty glass represents a well-known street-seller whose cry was 'Buy my ballads and I'll give you a glass of gin for nothing.' At the prosperous pawnbroker's, a carpenter pledges his saw for drink and a woman her pots and pans. Horrors are everywhere: a woman in a drunken stupor lets the baby she has been suckling fall headlong into the alley below; a barber, ruined by liquor, has hanged himself; and a drunken madman has impaled a child on a stake.

77

The Invasion—England

AT the beginning of the Seven Years War in 1756, the French command made plans for the capture of Minorca, then regarded as second only to Gibraltar in strategic importance for Britain, and, as a cover, assembled a large force of men and landing craft on the northern shores of France to simulate preparations for an invasion of the English shores. The threat threw the government, under the Duke of Newcastle, into a state of panic. This situation forms the background to Hogarth's print, which was a patriotic appeal to his countrymen to rally to the defence of their homes. In front of an inn, whose sign bears an equestrian representation of the Duke of Cumberland, the victor of Culloden, the artist displays the beef-bred English cheerfully preparing to repel the invader. A grenadier is painting on the wall a caricature of Louis XV from whose mouth issues the words: 'You take a my fine ships, you be de Pirate, you be de Teef, me send my grand Armies, & hang you all, Morblu,' an allusion to French complaints of English depredations on their shipping. A young woman measures the width of the grenadier's shoulders with her apron, and another puts her finger on the point of her fork, as an indication of the sharpness of the sailor's weapons. On a table loaded with beef lies the song 'Rule Britannia,' and in the foreground a fifer plays 'God save great George our King.' To the right, a sergeant measures with his cane and halberd a young recruit, who raises himself on the tips of his toes to reach the required height.

The Cockpit

COCKFIGHTING, that characteristically English institution, was a very ancient game, and as the 'sport of kings' was often attached to royal palaces. Hogarth portrayed the Royal Cockpit, taken down in 1816, which stood at some steps leading from Birdcage Walk into Dartmouth Street, Westminster. Watching the cocks dying in the sand is a motley crowd of human beings, noblemen, pickpockets, butchers, rat-catchers, jockeys and chimney-sweeps, shoulder to shoulder, and yet completely isolated, so much is each prisoner of his own passions. Over the general pandemonium presides a figure stranger and more solitary than any Hogarth depicted: Lord Albemarle Bertie, a younger son of the Duke of Ancaster, whose passion for the sport was more singular in that he was completely blind. His hat before him, brimming over with banknotes, he frenziedly arranges bets, as an unscrupulous neighbour steals a note. The reflection on the table is the shadow of a man who has received the customary punishment for defaulters—being hoisted up to the ceiling in a basket. From this exalted position he is desperately attempting to continue to bet by pledging his watch. Outside the barrier, a French marquis takes snuff as he watches the fight with interest and the audience with contempt. On the wall is a portrait of Nan Rawlins, the famous cock-handler, nicknamed the 'Duchess of Deptford,' who was a well-known figure at Newmarket.

The Stage Coach; or, Country Inn Yard

THE state of eighteenth-century roads was appalling. The inhabitants of each parish through which a road passed were responsible for its upkeep by means of unpaid labour, but, with no outside supervision, roads were hardly ever repaired. For most of the year they were a wilderness of mud and swamp, and men as well as horses were actually drowned in potholes on the Great North Road. Travel was slow—a stage coach was five or six days creeping a hundred miles—and dangerous—roads were infested with highway robbers. A stage coach usually carried six passengers inside, the humble being allowed to cling to the luggage on the roof.

Hogarth's engraving shows us an old country inn, just before the departure of the stage. An enormously fat woman is being shoved in by her husband, and a man of equally generous proportions waits

for his turn, completely ignoring the small hump-backed postillion, who vainly endeavours to extract the customary vail. Behind the vehicle, an old woman is ensconced in the basket. Two men are on the roof, a moody French footman and a sailor from the *Centurion*, one of Anson's ships which had distinguished herself in the action off Cape Finisterre in May 1747.

As the stout hostess in the bow window vigorously rings a bell to summon the passengers, the landlord is presenting a bill to an election agent, from whose pocket protrudes a copy of the Act against bribery at elections. The galleries of the inn-yard are filled with spectators watching a mock election procession carrying the effigy of a large baby holding a child's rattle—a reference to the 1747 Essex election when the Hon. John Child Tylney stood for the county, aged barely twenty, and was ridiculed with the cry 'No Old Baby.'